Creative Homes

Interiors and Design in the Netherlands

gestalten

CONTENTS

4
Dutch Design and its Relevance Today

12
Barn Revival

26
Pretty in Pink

36
Coach House

46
Black Outside/Color Inside

58
Architect's Dwelling

66
Converted Butcher's Shop

72
Canal House

80
Converted Urban Dairy

94
Converted Boy's School

102
Row House

108
Courage Houseboat

118
Holiday House

128
Flower Farm

140
Farm Conversion

152
Converted Cheese Farm

160
Industrial Loft

170
Garage Conversion

186
Het Katshuis

202
Farmhouse

214
Converted Factory

DUTCH DESIGN AND ITS RELEVANCE TODAY

These 20 homes of designers, architects, and artists dissolve the boundary between work and life into a blend of creativity. Here, the inhabitants use their living spaces as extensions of their professional endeavors.

Dutch design peaked as a global brand in the 1990s and early 2000s for its boldness and playful irreverence. These decades were marked by a relentless sense of open-mindedness and positivity following the fall of the Berlin Wall in 1989 and the anticipation of a new millennium. A lot has changed since then. Today's world is grappling with challenges such as climate change, biodiversity loss, and social injustice. That leads to the question as to whether Dutch design is still relevant in this age.

Creative Homes showcases the face of contemporary Dutch design by exploring a selection of extraordinary residences, revealing how today's creatives are shaping and redefining design in the Netherlands. The selection includes modern apartments, converted warehouses, rustic farmhouses, and a sleek houseboat, all photographed by René van der Hulst.

Creative Homes showcases the face of contemporary Dutch design by exploring a selection of extraordinary residences, revealing how today's creatives are shaping and redefining design in the Netherlands.

What distinguishes these residences is the individuals behind them: the designers, architects, artists, and makers who use their living spaces as extensions of their professional endeavors. Each profile invites readers into a world where personal narrative intersects with professional expertise, dissolving the boundary between work and life into a seamless blend of creativity. For instance, the farmhouse of product designers Kiki van Eijk and Joost van Bleiswijk illustrates how personal history and artistic vision coalesce into a unique living environment. Similarly, the townhouse of architect Thomas Bedaux showcases how simplicity and functionality create a serene space reflecting professional philosophies.

Rooted in traditions valuing simplicity and practicality while embracing experimentation, Dutch design still profoundly influences living spaces in the Netherlands and elsewhere. Iconic movements like De Stijl and Droog set foundational standards in modern design. This influence is evident in the featured homes, where form and function combine with respect for craftsmanship and materiality.

These residences represent a broad spectrum of styles. Some dwellings, such as the repurposed urban dairy of designer Frans Schrofer, blend historical elements with modern interventions. Others, like the houseboat of Sjoerd and Jacoline Ribberink, capture a minimalist aesthetic emphasizing open spaces and natural light. A common thread unites these homes: purposeful decision-making behind every object. Every component—from the furniture and lighting to the art—has been carefully considered to reflect the inhabitants' personalities. Sustainable materials and practices highlight a commitment to environmental responsibility. Many creatives incorporate reclaimed materials or collaborate with local artisans, supporting the community and reducing environmental impact.

An emphasis on functionality and environmental performance without sacrificing aesthetic appeal resonates with contemporary practices valuing sustainability, practicality, and beauty. By delving into these spaces, readers will gain insight into how to apply design principles in their everyday lives, encouraging a thoughtful approach to creating one's environment.

By showcasing the diversity and ingenuity of Dutch homes today, *Creative Homes* affirms the relevance of Dutch design in contemporary culture and its capacity to continue to shape the future of living spaces.

These 20 homes address the question of Dutch design's continued relevance and offer a compelling argument for its ongoing vitality. They demonstrate that Dutch design has evolved, integrating today's societal challenges while maintaining core principles of innovation and functionality. The creativity evident in these 20 homes reflects a living tradition that continues to adapt and inspire.

The following pages offer an intimate look into spaces where professional and private life converge in an inhabitable space. These profiles reveal the homes and the human stories behind them, demonstrating that a good home always expresses personal history. By showcasing the diversity and ingenuity of Dutch homes today, *Creative Homes* affirms the relevance of Dutch design in contemporary culture and its capacity to continue to shape the future of living spaces.

David Keuning

Barn Revival, Eindhoven. *Designed and inhabited by* Kiki van Eijk & Joost van Bleiswijk

A VESSEL FOR CHANGE

When product designers Kiki van Eijk and Joost van Bleiswijk visited a garden center in the vicinity of Eindhoven some time ago, they were immediately smitten by a small piece of land around the corner. They envisioned building a new house there, but when they made an offer, it turned out that the opportunity had passed by. On the plot next door, however, stood a dilapidated former farm building held together by scaffolding. This time the couple took their chance, made an offer without the land even being for sale, and were lucky.

What followed was a lengthy renovation process. The presence of woodworm and dry rot meant that the internal timber structure had to be completely replaced. Van Eijk and van Bleiswijk took the opportunity to add a few modest interventions, the most striking of which is a "light catcher": a 16.5 × 16.5 ft. (5 × 5 m) window facing the garden that opens the otherwise quite insular barn to the outside. The result was a generous indoor space—28 ft. (8.5 m) tall at the point of the ridge, divided in two by a large fireplace.

This huge space needed a lot of furniture; more than the pair had in their previous, much smaller home. Van Eijk and van Bleiswijk slowly filled it with a mixture of design pieces and second-hand objects. Of course, they also included a few pieces of their own design, but not too many. The blue-and-white carpet in the living room, for instance, is van Eijk's. Nothing is set in stone, though, and part of the charm of this place is that there is room for continuous evolution.

The PP124 rocking chair by Hans J. Wegner offers a perfect view of the garden. The carpet on the floor was designed by van Eijk for Nodus; van Bleiswijk designed the oversized Construction floor lamp for Moooi. The six chairs around the dining-room table were made by van Bleiswijk himself.

BARN REVIVAL, EINDHOVEN

The green kitchen island comes from an old workshop at
Philips Electronics in Eindhoven and was given a new countertop
with an integrated stove. It is one of many examples
of recycling and upcycling that can be found in the house.

Tile Stove Big, designed by Dick van Hoff for Royal Tichelaar, in Makkum, was produced by Weltevree and now heats a cozy room in this former farm building. The many artworks on the wall were made by graduates from the Design Academy Eindhoven.

Pretty in Pink, Arnhem. *Designed and inhabited by* Chantal Assinck & Tom Klomberg

LITTLE PINK HOUSE

When location scout Chantal Assinck and HR-manager Tom Klomberg moved into a 624 sq. ft. (58 m²) apartment in the city center of Arnhem, it had already lost all of its original details in a devastating fire in the 1990s. This gave the couple free reign to renovate the apartment to their own taste. The building, built in 1955 in a functionalist style, had retained its most important qualities, including large windows that flood the space with natural light.

Assinck and Klomberg's main decision was an uncompromising one: they decided to paint the whole apartment pink. Not just the walls, but also the doors, door frames, ceilings, and cabinets. They first hired a contractor to gut the apartment, pulling down false ceilings and removing a wall between the kitchen and the living room to create a single, spacious area with daylight flowing in from both sides.

After the contractor was done, Assinck and Klomberg took over and did the finishing by themselves. With cabinets from Ikea and simple white tiles from a local DIY store, they custom-built a spacious kitchen reminiscent of the famous tile designs that were part of the Droog collection in the '90s. The nifty little bathroom served as the exception to the rule and was executed in green. The couple also built many of the cabinets and other pieces of furniture themselves.

This small apartment shows how much can be achieved with relatively modest means. One clear design principle, rigorously executed, is all that is needed to create a home that stands out.

The small apartment houses a large number of design objects.
Frank Gehry's Wiggle side chair in the corner of the room
is complemented by a miniature version of the Red and Blue Chair
by Gerrit Rietveld on the wall cabinet.

Coach House, Den Bosch. *Designed and inhabited by* Ruud van den Akker & Roel Vaessen

ECLECTIC PATCHWORK HOME

Ruud van den Akker and Roel Vaessen are co-founders of IXXI, a company that produces modular wall decorations in a huge range of sizes and prints. No surprise, then, that a specimen adorns a wall in their own house in Den Bosch. A wide-eyed, pink-and-yellow fish drawn by 18th-century naturalist Marcus Elieser Bloch, from the collection of London's Natural History Museum, peeks into the couple's large kitchen. In many ways, the drawing is representative of the house as a whole—a colorful patchwork of individual parts that together form a cohesive whole.

This building is a former coach house, erected in 1900, in the center of Den Bosch. When van den Akker and Vaessen bought it, a renovation by the previous owner remained unfinished, which meant the couple had ample opportunity to make the 2,260 sq. ft. (210 m²) structure their own. Vaessen, who trained as a graphic designer, personally drew up the renovation plans, and while a contractor took care of major interventions, the couple worked on the finishes themselves.

In a large extension at the back of the 23-foot-wide (7 m) house is an open-plan kitchen with a large glass wall facing the 3,230 sq. ft. (300 m²) garden. It features a kitchen island designed by Vaessen (an enthusiastic cook), based on cabinets from Ikea. The former back wall of the coach house was kept intact and is now separated from the extension by a strip of glass in the ceiling. In the living room at the front of the house, a stairwell gives access to the bedrooms on the upper floors. The interior is an eclectic and happy explosion of colors and shapes that never clash, thanks to a neutral background. A little like IXXI, in fact.

The bookshelves that hide the stairwell to the upper floors were custom-made from Polish pine. The Lot couch was designed by Studio Parade for Vrienden. The couple drew the coffee table themselves. The Katrijn chair was designed by Floris Hovers, also for Vrienden.

Black Outside/Color Inside, Tilburg. *Designed and inhabited by* Julien & Malon Arts

BLACK BOX, COLORFUL CUBE

Graphic designer Julien Arts and children's clothing designer Malon Arts came across the 1980s house they now inhabit by chance, after picking up their daughter Clélie from day care one day. It was not for sale at the time, but it immediately struck them as the perfect canvas for their colorful daydreams about a future home. Lo and behold, the building came on the market just two weeks later. It was meant to be. The house was well maintained but needed an update. Brown carpets and curtains were taken out, to be replaced by color and light. The first big project was the stairwell to the first floor, for which artist Ward Wijnant designed a new banister. The couple also involved other artists from their network. They collaborated with Nynke Tynagel (formerly of Studio Job) on the graphic pattern designed for the front-door windows. The kitchen walls were covered with colorful ceramic tiles produced by Gilles de Brock. Julien Arts himself was responsible for the design of the white railing on the rooftop terrace at the rear side of the building, which boasts an intricate lacelike pattern. At the couple's request, and in stark contrast to the colorful interior, the exterior walls of the house were painted pitch-black.

Inside, the furniture is a happy hodgepodge of design pieces. To name just a few, the living room boasts a Plain Clay floor lamp by Maarten Baas, a green Chubby chair by Dirk van der Kooij, and a Spine armchair designed for Arco by Burkhard Vogtherr. A very happy trio indeed.

A bright-blue Bold bench, designed by Big-Game for Moustache, is the centerpiece of the spacious entrance hall. A custom artwork by Martin Lorenz is mounted on the ceiling. Under the stairs are a Twisted chair by Ward Wijnant and the Comtoise wall clock by Alessi and Studio Job.

The ceramic tiles in the kitchen feature colorful graphic patterns and were produced by Gilles de Brock. On the Bora stove is an Alessi kettle 3909, originally designed by Michael Graves and reimagined by Virgil Abloh. The salt and pepper grinders and the metal storage containers are from the Hay collection.

Architect's Dwelling, Tilburg. *Designed by* Bedaux de Brouwer Architects.
Inhabited by Thomas Bedaux & Marthe Nagengast

ALL IN THE FAMILY

For any architect, designing your own home is a litmus test. When you are your own client, you have the freedom to do anything you want. At the same time, there is the pressure to do everything right: the house also serves as your business card.

Thomas Bedaux, third-generation architect in the well-known Dutch firm Bedaux de Brouwer, succeeded brilliantly in this task. For a plot in a 1930s neighborhood east of downtown Tilburg, he designed a spacious detached family home. The minimalist exterior conceals a carefully designed interior in which story height and window placement are matched to the function of each room. The living quarters on the ground floor give access to the south-facing garden. The living room is one step lower than the dining room, giving it a taller ceiling height than rooms in the rest of the house. On the street side is a playroom with lower than usual ceilings. This not only matches the spatial experience of the children, it allows the design studio above to have a higher ceiling. A north-facing window gives the studio the gentle and consistent daylight that it requires.

Bedaux designed many small details himself, including the mailbox, house number, and door handles—the last a reinterpretation of a design by his grandfather. The result is a practical yet highly aesthetic family home where the architect can receive friends and potential clients with confidence.

The three children's bedrooms are on the top floor.
Gray, cast-concrete floors and white walls provide a quiet
base for cheerful children's toys. Under the glass bell jar
is a miniature rendering of the Bedaux-Nagengast family.

Converted Butcher's Shop, Tilburg. *Designed by* Ed Bergers Architects. *Inhabited by* Rens Alta

PRIVATE AND PLAYFUL

When Rens Alta bought a former butcher's shop and butchery in Tilburg in 1996, he housed his furniture store Alta Design in the shop and used the former butchery behind as a warehouse. In the beginning, Alta Design focused primarily on antiques, flea-market finds, and decorative interior objects, but over time the emphasis shifted to arts and crafts from the 1950s to the 1970s.

The butcher's shop had been built in about 1914. In the butchery behind the store, meat had been cut, boned, and smoked. When Alta divorced in 2014, he ended up with the store and the warehouse, which architect Ed Bergers subsequently converted into a home. Alta started living there in 2019.

Because the house is enclosed by a garden on one side and an alley on the other, it is quite secluded. Nevertheless, there is no shortage of light. High-set windows allow daylight to flood in. A tall ceiling and a loft with a newly installed steel staircase do the rest. The simple, efficient layout—the total area of the house is 800 sq. ft. (75 m^2)—is both charming and clear: kitchen and storage on the ground floor, bathroom on the mezzanine, living room and bedroom on the upper floor.

Alta assembled the interior using objects from his store, and things change from time to time. He says he does not cling to a particular style. The 19th-century marble sink in the bathroom is as dear to him as the 1960s cascade lamp, designed by Gino Sarfatti for Arteluce. This laissez-faire aesthetic produces a pleasant and casual home, hidden from outside glances yet in the middle of the city.

Rens Alta's home is a quiet sanctuary, tucked away in the middle of the city of Tilburg. The tall windows above the kitchen overlook an impressive, 100-year-old beech tree.

Canal House, Amsterdam. *Designed and inhabited by* Marc van Nederpelt & Merel Bunnik

TIMELESS DESIGN TREASURES

Marc van Nederpelt, cofounder of Dutch furniture brand DUM, and Modefabriek event director Merel Bunnik moved to this 17th-century canal house in 2013. The couple had bought the house from an elderly man who had been living there for more than 40 years, following a renovation in the 1970s. Although the house was in a state of disrepair, it retained many original features.

The house was listed, which meant that van Nederpelt and Bunnik had to adhere to many strict rules. Big changes were out of the question, but the mezzanine in the living room had been installed during the 1970's renovation and could be kept. Among other things, the couple installed new wooden floors, replastered and painted all walls, and made sure that new pipes and wiring remained out of sight. They also designed the custom-built kitchen themselves. The marble countertop goes very well with the old floor in the monumental hallway. The interior combines pieces from the DUM collection with vintage furniture. Bunnik's favorite piece is the Elda armchair by Joe Colombo, which belonged to her grandfather. Van Nederpelt is most attached to the round Beech Connect table and Beech chairs, which were the very first prototypes that DUM produced. Together van Nederpelt and Bunnik have created an impressive house that harbors many fond memories for them, both privately and professionally.

CANAL HOUSE, AMSTERDAM

The living room has a ceiling height of 13 ft. (4 m), lending
the room a very grand atmosphere. The Pleat pendant lights were
designed by Dum for Hollands Licht. Jan des Bouvrie designed
the vintage sofa under the windows.

Converted Urban Dairy, The Hague. *Designed and inhabited by* Frans Schrofer & Sonia Sin

A CREATIVE LEGACY

Frans Schrofer's home reflects the creative legacy of his family. Born into a lineage of artistic talent, his father, Willem Schrofer, was a painter and teacher, while his mother, Hannie Bal, was a textile artist, and his uncle Jan cofounded the Cirkel Group, a furniture factory. Rather than stepping out of this creative shadow, Frans embraced it, founding Studio Schrofer in 1984. Together with his partner Sonia Sin and their design team, he specializes in contemporary furniture for international brands.

Schrofer's home, a historic urban dairy he purchased in 1984, is a testament to his family history. The 4,300 sq. ft. (400 m²) complex, once neglected, has been meticulously reconstructed and expanded, reflecting the designer's past and present life. The house is filled with paintings by his father, including a cherished 1948 self-portrait, creating a living museum of family art. Schrofer often discovers undocumented works by his father, adding to the home's evolving narrative.

The furniture throughout the house evokes professional memories. A white leather sofa in the living room represents Schrofer's first design for Natuzzi Italia. A green sofa prototype for Gealux sits in an adjacent room, and dining chairs from various clients occupy the kitchen and dining room. Each piece tells a story of his design journey, making the house a true "memory lane" of both family and creativity.

Frans Schrofer's father, Willem, is present throughout the house, depicted in drawings, paintings, and book publications. Willem taught at the Royal Academy of Art in The Hague, where one of his students, Hannie Bal, eventually became his wife.

CONVERTED URBAN DAIRY, THE HAGUE

A 1928 Motobécane bike stands in the hallway, though Schrofer rides
a Moto 6.5 designed by Philippe Starck. A partial view of a
self-portrait of his father from 1959 adds to the artistic narrative.

CONVERTED URBAN DAIRY, THE HAGUE

The house is a labyrinth of stairwells and hidden spaces, creating a sense of discovery at every turn. At the heart of the home is a central courtyard that serves as an oasis of tranquility in the city.

Converted Boy's School, Tilburg. *Designed and inhabited by* Sigrid Calon & Gerko Koenen

CLASS IN SESSION

Visual artist Sigrid Calon and sustainability manager Gerko Koenen live in an 1895 former Catholic boys' school in Tilburg. After years of searching for a suitable property to serve as both a home and a studio, Calon found the property more or less by accident. Not available for sale, it was instead owned by a contractor who had bought it from the church council and who planned to convert it into housing. However, the contractor had a full order book and was willing to resell the property to Calon and Koenen. Since Koenen works for a contractor himself, the pair were able to do the remodeling themselves. The building gained underfloor heating, a heat pump, and solar panels. The renovation revealed beautiful original features, such as the concrete ceiling and the profiled brackets in the current living room.

The remodel resulted in a large, industrial space with high ceilings that showcases both furniture pieces and artwork. One wall in the open-plan kitchen is completely covered with works by artist friends. Between the artworks hangs a framed, flat-screen television that offers a slideshow of images of Calon's own work during the day. Trained as a textile artist, she also makes books and prints, among other things. Her studio is located in the former theater hall of the parish house: a rise in the floor indicates the former stage. The dark space has been transformed into a generous studio with north-facing skylights. They provide the even light needed to see works of art clearly. So, with a lot of dedication and expertise, Calon and Koenen have created a beautiful space in which living and working can merge harmoniously.

The two black seats in the open-plan kitchen are from the 1970s, possibly from Artifort, and were owned by Calon's mother. The dining chairs belonged to Calon's grandmother. Behind the arches to the right is the living room.

CONVERTED BOY'S SCHOOL, TILBURG

Behind the dahlias is an extension to the building that formerly served as office space. It is now the living room. Calon and Koenen removed false ceilings and inserted a large skylight. The bedroom is in the attic. Trusses had to be removed in order to allow the inhabitants to walk here.

Row House, Tilburg. *Designed and inhabited by* Robbie Bensing & Dannieke Bensing-Diepenmaat

THE NATURE OF LIVING

That a renovation can turn a terraced house, built in 1997, into an original and personal living space is proven by interior designer Robbie Bensing and interior stylist Dannieke Bensing-Diepenmaat of design firm Wolfpak Studio. This radical renovation of their own home in Tilburg took three months and included, among other things, moving a staircase and a large number of walls. This created space on the ground floor for a large, eat-in kitchen, which is connected to the living room on the second floor via a void on the garden side. Apart from the kitchen itself, which was designed by the couple and executed in dark oak, the eye-catcher on the ground floor is the ceiling covered with ash slats, which Bensing laid himself. The parapet of the mezzanine is clad with the same, emphasizing the height of the room. The wooden ceiling contrasts beautifully with the gray, cast-concrete floor, which, with the white walls, provides a neutral base for the interior, which features a mid-century wall cabinet by Pastoe and contemporary furniture in natural, earth-toned materials.

A 16.5-foot-high (5 m), south-facing glass facade on the garden side allows daylight to penetrate deep into the home. Thanks to this, the heating hardly ever needs to be turned on and the sunlight creates beautiful shadows on the high white walls. Simple things like this make living in the house a pleasure for its owners.

The backyard faces south and is landscaped with fig trees and olive trees. The concrete terrace is on the same level as the dining-room floor so that indoors and outdoors flow together almost seamlessly.

Courage Houseboat, Utrecht. *Designed by* Lars Courage & Gerrit Holdijk.
Inhabited by Sjoerd & Jacoline Ribberink

HOUSE OF STEEL

Architect Lars Courage is well known for his sleek, industrial buildings. He uses steel structures and cladding, often in black, for houses as well as offices, lending them a minimalist yet bold touch. This houseboat in black steel is a floating addition to his otherwise land-based portfolio.

The clients, Sjoerd and Jacoline Ribberink, previously lived in a small house in the old town center of Utrecht, a listed building full of charm and accompanying defects. The couple wanted more space and greater comfort, so decided to buy an old houseboat with a mooring spot and to replace the existing houseboat with a new 2,690 sq. ft. (250 m²), two-story version. In addition to the architect they involved interior designer Gerrit Holdijk. Where Courage provided a black background, Holdijk added color—mainly blue, yellow, and pink. The structure, consisting of a steel framework with sandwich panels and glass, meant that ducts for utilities had to be carefully planned; all sockets, for instance, are integrated in the steel columns. The cast-concrete floors and large pieces of furniture, such as the kitchen island with its solid steel countertop, had to be taken into account in the overall weight distribution of the floating structure, making a tight collaboration between architect and interior architect essential. The final result proves that it was also a very fruitful one.

The contrast between the black framing and the colorful interior makes for a balanced and peaceful space that gives center stage to the daylight and the rippling reflections of the water. A wooden block in the middle of the boat serves as a podium upstairs and provides ample storage space below, its rich wood grain countering the smooth steel and concrete surfaces. What's not to love?

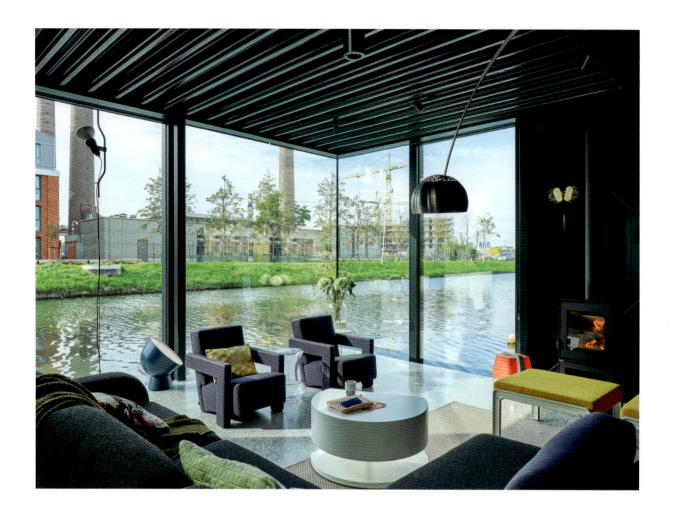

The houseboat is moored alongside Merwede Canal, which separates an early 20th-century neighborhood from former industrial estates on the other side, which are currently being redeveloped. It is a fitting environment for the bold black vessel.

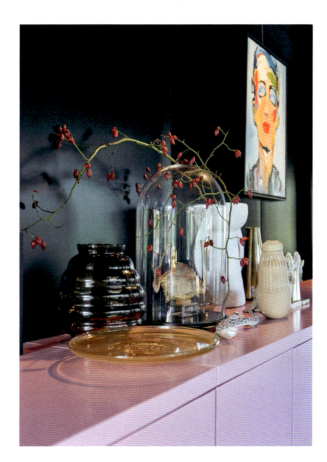
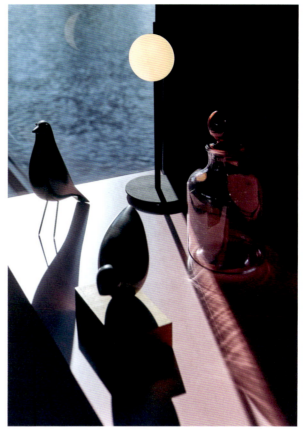

The kitchen combines yellow accents with a 20-foot-long (6 m) row of pink wall cabinets. Steel walls and ceilings allow all paintings and light armatures to be hung using magnets, keeping surfaces intact and making a rehang a breeze.

Holiday House, Arnhem. *Designed by* Sander van Schaik & Robert-Jan de Kort.
Inhabited by Joris Bak & Astrid Bergman

UNDER THE RADAR

Buitenplaats Koningsweg, near De Hoge Veluwe National Park, close to the city of Arnhem, is an estate with a somewhat dark past. During the Second World War, the site was home to the barracks of a German airbase, Fliegerhorst Deelen. To hide the aircraft hangars and other structures on the site from the Allies, the Germans disguised the buildings as barns and planted fake cows in the fields to reinforce the impression.

Those days are now long gone and the former base barely visible. Instead, the site has been transformed into an estate where artists and other creatives live and work. The most recent addition consists of 11 small vacation homes arising from a design competition in 2021. Tech company director Joris Bak and communications adviser Astrid Bergman approached architects Sander van Schaik and Robert-Jan de Kort, having read about their design for a villa inspired by a boulder. They asked for a small, tranquil retreat that would encourage them to do nothing.

The architects came up with a design titled "under the radar," referring not only to the camouflaged buildings that were once on the site, but also to the nearby radar tower. The holiday home has a steel A-frame—a structure often seen in mountain huts because of its simple but sturdy qualities. The black steel structure is reminiscent of the stealth attack aircraft F-117 Nighthawk, developed in the 1980s to remain invisible to radar using stealth technology. Bak and Bergman celebrated their first vacation in their retreat in Christmas 2023. It allows them to do exactly what they wanted: nothing.

The architects integrated nearly all furniture, cabinets, and storage spaces into the design. Weather permitting, the indoor bench can be used from outside, making the terrace part of the living space.

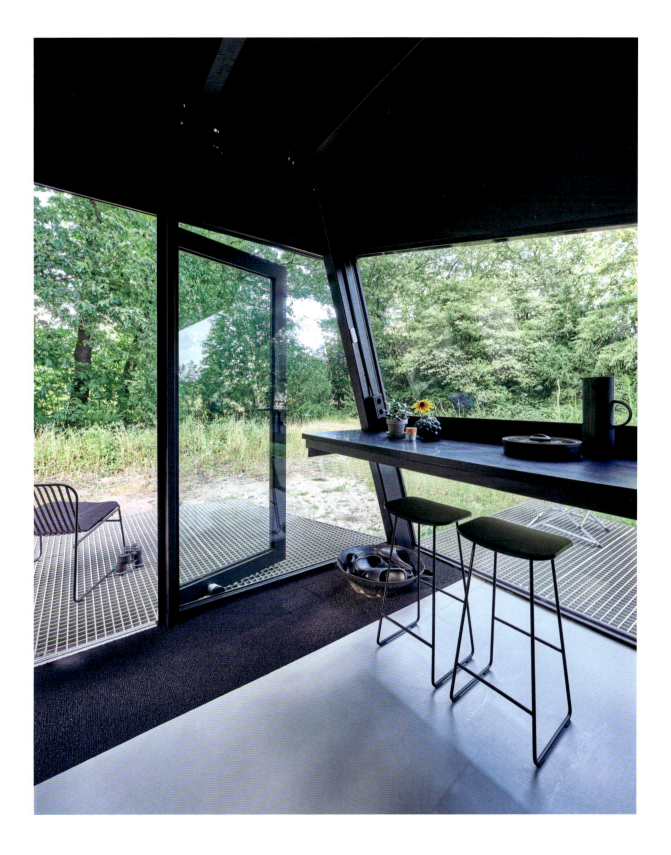

A skylight crowns the double bed on a mezzanine at the top of the A-frame, allowing residents to enjoy the surrounding treetops, the sky, and the stars at night. Green glass vase by Klaas Kuiken.

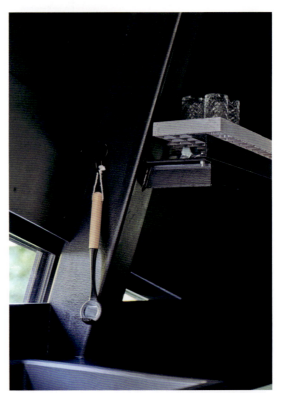

Flower Farm, Moergestel. *Designed by* WillemsenU & Carolien Schrievers.
Inhabited by Carolien & Lucas Schrievers

FLOWERY GARDEN GALORE

Interior stylist and florist Carolien Schrievers and her entrepreneur husband Lucas moved to an old, thatched farmhouse in the Brabant village of Moergestel about two decades ago. Gradually they started converting the property: the current living areas used to be stables. At the back of the house, perpendicular to the original building, they erected a new garden house that is clad in western red cedar and features storage, a study, a guest bedroom, and an outdoor kitchen. The main feature is the stunning garden which covers nearly 2 acres (0.8 hectares) of land and includes a flower garden, orchard, and swimming pond. Schrievers regularly opens it up to visitors, with tours and flower-picking days, making sure it is enjoyed and appreciated by other people besides her own family.

Back to the main house. During the renovations, bedrooms and a bathroom were installed under the thatched roof. The ground floor now houses a living room on the street side and a large kitchen and dining room to the rear. There are few walls on the ground floor and the timber ceilings were painted white, giving the living quarters a spacious look that is enhanced by the windows, many of which were enlarged to bring in more daylight and offer expanded views of the garden. The living room features wide, wooden floorboards while the kitchen has a tiled floor and opens up directly to the garden. The interior decoration is quite eclectic, offering a mix between old and new. In that sense, garden and house complement one another perfectly.

The dining-room table by Piet Hein Eek is surrounded by mismatched chairs. On the table, a striking ceramic Citron vase by Des Pots steals the show. The walls are painted in various shades of green by Ressource.

The kitchen at the rear of the house opens up to the garden. The Polder sofa and the decorative vase in the corner are both by Hella Jongerius—the sofa for Vitra and the vase for Ikea.

Farm Conversion, Berkel-Enschot. *Designed and inhabited by* Rob van Trier & Sandra van Groezen

BON VIVANT ABODE

Before painter Rob van Trier moved into his present abode, dating from 1781, the building had served not only as a farmhouse, but also as a brothel and even a laboratory producing synthetic drugs. After the latter was discovered and dismantled, little was left of the building's former glory. Rob van Trier, who urgently needed housing and was not deterred by the dilapidated state of the building. He moved in, initially as a property guardian, and slowly started to repair basic amenities. When the owner decided to split the farm into three sections and put them up for sale, van Trier bought the middle part. A more thorough renovation followed, taking three and a half years. Whenever van Trier was short of money, he funded the renovation by selling some of his paintings.

The results are impressive. The former farm is now the comfortable home of a colorful bon vivant. What had once been a pigsty at the rear of the building now serves as a kitchen, painting studio, and art gallery. At the front, where the cowshed used to be, are a hallway and living room. The attic, once used as a hayloft, now houses a bedroom and bathroom.

The house is a treasure trove of visual delights. Apart from the ubiquitous art on the walls—almost all by van Trier himself—there are many objects that elicit wonder and curiosity. Among them is a Jules Verne–like stove in the kitchen that van Trier made out of a 1901 pressure vessel. Creativity that ignores conventional boundaries between art disciplines: that is what this house is all about.

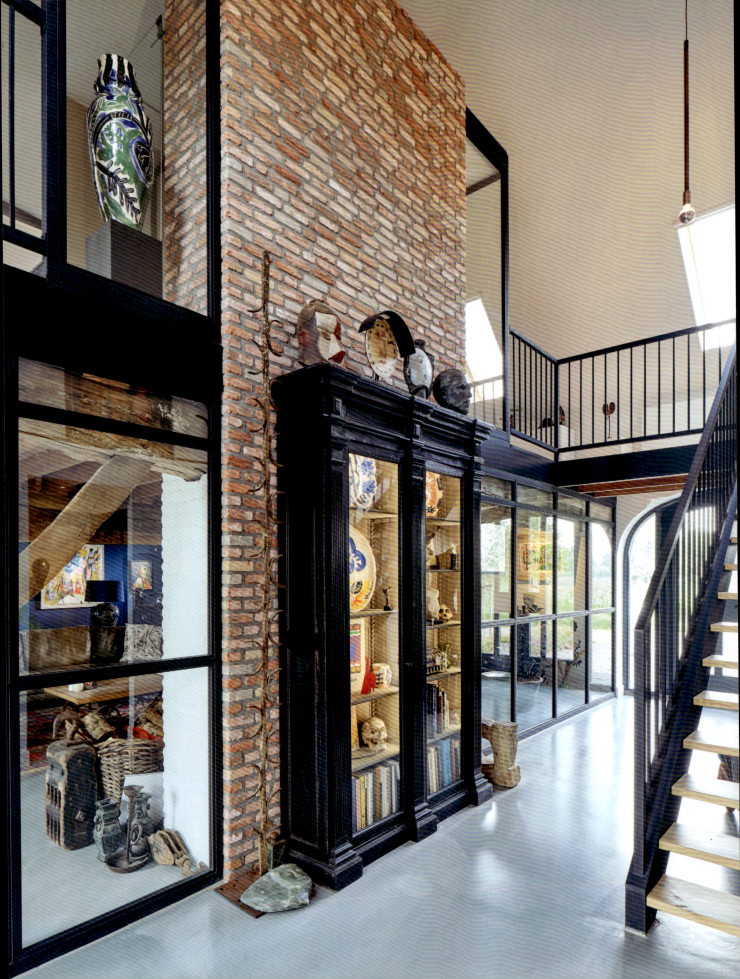

A brick core in the middle of the house serves as a chimney for a stove on the ground floor. Large and small artworks are exhibited in a glass case reminiscent of a 17th-century cabinet of curiosities.

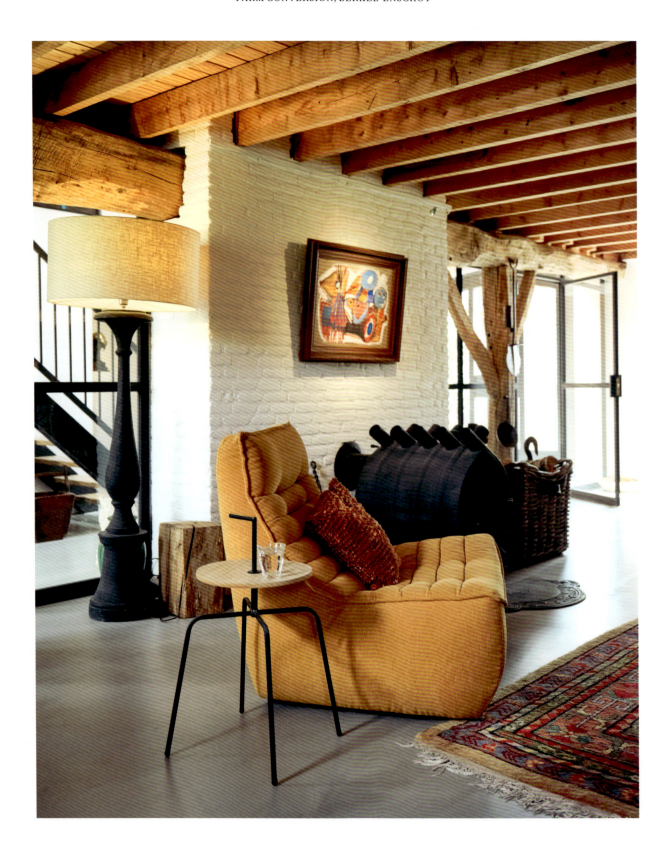

A glass-roofed passageway connects the bedroom in the attic to the kitchen at the rear of the house. The double-height kitchen also serves as a painting studio and art gallery; van Trier sells his work from home. The wall color is French ultramarine blue.

Converted Cheese Farm, Breukelen. *Designed and inhabited by* Alex Groot Jebbink & Sonja Werners

RUSTIC CHARM REDEFINED

Alex Groot Jebbink and Sonja Werners live in an old farmhouse together with Sonja's twin sister and her husband. The idea to look for a joint home arose in a café a few years ago. Neither couple has children but both wanted companionship—and security should one of them ever need care.

The four of them found a 19th-century former cheese farm near Utrecht that was in poor condition but offered enough space for two couples. Groot Jebbink and Werners now live in a former barn at the back of the property, and the twin sister and her husband inhabit the old living quarters at the front. Between the two, there was enough space for a large event hall that can be used for such things as theater performances—the field in which the twin sister and her husband are active—or book presentations (Werners herself works as an event organizer).

Groot Jebbink carried out the renovation himself, in cooperation with a contractor with whom he works frequently. Having initially studied mechanical engineering, after a ten-year career with the Dutch railroad, Groot Jebbink decided to change course and studied interior and furniture design. After graduating, he became a product designer of tables, then lighting. He designs interiors as well, and felt honor-bound to remodel his own home himself. This also made the whole project financially feasible. The result is a beautiful and practical home that radiates a sense of joy, creativity, and warmth.

Werners and Groot Jebbink's bedroom is in the attic. When the couple bought the farm, the roof trusses were found to have woodworm; they were treated and the roof was completely renewed. On the balustrade around the stairs is a collection of Vitra miniatures.

CONVERTED CHEESE FARM, BREUKELEN

The house lies in an idyllic location in the countryside near Breukelen, close to Utrecht. A large garden offers ample space for relaxation and gives the inhabitants the feeling that they are permanently on holiday.

Industrial Loft, Maastricht. *Designed by* Janneke Hulshof & Katarina Labathova.
Inhabited by Remko ten Barge & Marjon ten Barge-Kuenen

ROOM WITH A VIEW

Remko ten Barge, founder of energy supplier NieuweStroom in Maastricht, used to travel up and down weekly from his home in Utrecht, a drive of over 100 miles (160 km). This meant frequent stays in hotels and, eventually, a rental apartment. Soon his growing company needed more space and moved to the Eiffel Building in the heart of Maastricht. This former factory used to house the royal ceramics factory Sphinx. When ten Barge and his wife Marjon heard that 16 lofts would be realized on the top two floors of the building, their interest was piqued.

Their apartment is on the top floor, with access to a private roof terrace and great views over the center of Maastricht and the Meuse River. The couple asked Janneke Hulshof to design the space, an architect friend whom Remko has known since elementary school. Working with Katarina Labathova, Hulshof presented them with several options and they chose one described as the "multifunctional cube."

The cube in question, finished in oak veneer, separates the living room from the primary bedroom. This piece of furniture integrates part of the kitchen cabinets, a bedstead, and a walk-in closet. When the couple have guests, two ceiling-height doors close, creating a separate guest room. Because of the building's listed character, the concrete walls and ceilings may not be finished or painted, unless reversible false walls are used. Fortunately, the couple did not opt for this. The striking contrast between the raw concrete and the finely grained wood panels is exactly what makes this apartment utterly irresistible.

The 5.9×5.9 ft. (1.8×1.8 m) stainless-steel kitchen island is cleanly detailed. The smooth surfaces balance well with the gray concrete walls and ceilings. The green pendant Slender lamps and white vases by HKliving are via Mooi en Belle, Utrecht. The black-and-gold pendant lamp is by Faro Lighting.

When the doors to the bedstead are open, there is a direct view from the living room to the primary bedroom. A Vasca bathtub by Luca Sanitair is the centerpiece of the bedroom.

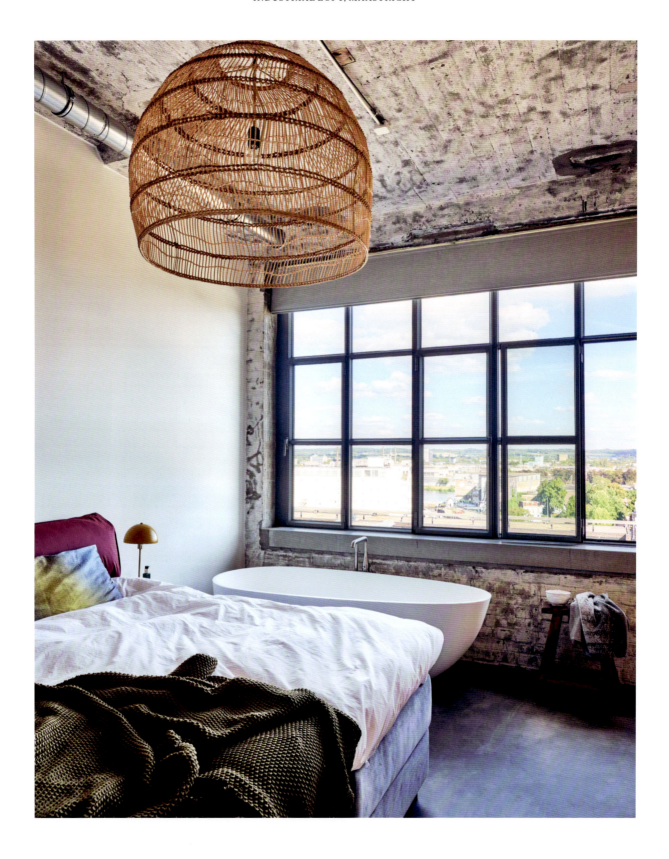

Garage Conversion, Den Bosch. *Designed by* Hilberink Bosch Architects & Studio Boot. *Inhabited by* Petra Janssen & Edwin Vollebergh

GARAGE TURNED HOME

Just over a decade ago, Petra Janssen and Edwin Vollebergh, owners of design firm Studio Boot, found a derelict garage in the town center of Den Bosch. Behind the 69-foot-wide (21 m) brick building was a huge, double-height hall, with a steel loadbearing structure and a mezzanine around a central void crowned by a large skylight. Despite its dilapidated state, Janssen and Vollebergh immediately saw its potential, and with the help of many friends, including Hilberink Bosch Architects and industrial designer Piet Hein Eek, they turned it into a family house and office space in which work and daily life are closely intertwined.

Today, the ground floor houses the design firm, with two office spaces at the front of the building. Glass walls offer a view of the double-height hall, which the team uses as a meeting room. At the back, giving access to a walled garden, is an open-plan kitchen, separated from the offices by a very long cupboard, made by Piet Hein Eek from a large number of second-hand doors. The mezzanine on the first floor is home to the living spaces, with separate bedrooms for the couple's two sons at the front. The primary bedroom and bathroom are in the attic on the second floor.

As vibrant as its owners, the interior comprises an eclectic mix of vintage design, second-hand furniture from thrift stores, and new objects. These objects echo the ideas behind the renovation of the building itself: almost all building materials, radiators, and other architectural elements were sourced from the structure as they found it. Underfloor heating and insulation keep the house comfortably warm.

The kitchen wall behind the oak chest serves as a display for the couple's collection of Delftware. The kitchen island is made of repurposed desks and the stove is integrated into the Piet Hein Eek–designed cupboard.

The second-hand Mercedes at the front door was a birthday present from Vollebergh to Janssen and serves as a reference to the building's former life as a garage. A skylight over the central void floods the hall with natural light.

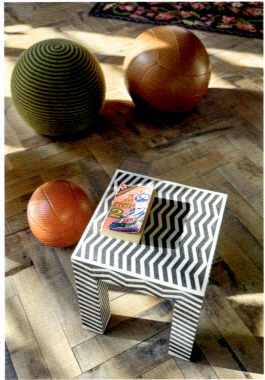

Het Katshuis, Kats. *Designed and inhabited by* Elly Prins & Remco van Heumen

PAST PERFECTED PRESENT

In the middle of the vast polders of Zeeland lies this fairy-tale estate. What, at first glance, appears to be an 18th-century mansion with an outbuilding is actually a 1930s home with a barn, but in reverse order: in 2016 designers Elly Prins and Remco van Heumen converted the barn into a country house, relegating the original home to a subordinate building. The result is a beautifully designed building complex that serves as a residence, design studio, and event venue.

During the conversion, Prins and van Heumen incorporated as many old building materials as possible, both from the Netherlands and abroad, yet did not compromise on modern comforts. For example, the old barn now has a steel structure, concrete floor, and underfloor heating. Prins and van Heumen also landscaped the garden. In a style appropriate to the renovated house, with long sightlines, they laid out an avenue of oaks with a fountain and an avenue of roses with thirteen rose arches.

The pair's main principle when designing interiors is that a room should be atmospheric, even when empty. As early as the construction phase, they paid attention to fireplaces and paneling and ceilings made of stucco or wood. Also characteristic of the design, the doors to the rooms are all in line with one another, a feature described as *enfilade*. It creates tranquility. Now, after more than eight years of remodeling and decorating, the house is completely finished. Prins and van Heumen have set their sights on a new project outside the Netherlands: Plymtree Manor in Devon, United Kingdom. Het Katshuis is for sale to a buyer who appreciates the couple's extraordinarily imaginative design philosophy.

In the gallery behind the garden room, two double doors lead to a very large veranda that offers a view of the classically laid out garden. Built-in benches and a vaulted ceiling lend the gallery a sense of days-gone-by grandeur.

The original home was turned into one big space that now serves as an open-plan kitchen, tea room, and sun room. Wood-clad walls give the space a barnlike atmosphere, which is enhanced by second-hand furniture.

Farmhouse, Hoogeloon. *Designed by* Ad Goossens. *Decorated and inhabited by* Micky Hoogendijk

PEACEFUL AND PRIVATE

Artist Micky Hoogendijk had already enjoyed a career as a celebrated photographer when she decided to take up sculpting a few years ago. Her new endeavor took off at a rapid pace: one sculpture from her first series in bronze, titled The Ones, was exhibited during the Venice Biennale in 2024. At the time of writing, Hoogendijk lives and works in Amsterdam, having moved there from the village of Hoogeloon, where she started working on The Ones in the socially distanced world of Covid.

Hoogendijk happened upon the former cowshed in Hoogeloon when she was exhibiting in the nearby village of Eersel in 2018. At the time she was living in Los Angeles. The shed, originally built in 1925, was being renovated by the owner, architect Ad Goossens, who lived down the road. Hoogendijk was immediately inspired by the peacefulness of the spot and approached the architect saying: "I will live here." And that's what happened. After moving in, it took a while for the place to feel like home, emotionally. It was large and empty and needed to be filled with Hoogendijk's belongings. Very little is new, and many objects have a history connected to the artist's own: artworks made by friends and furniture inherited from family members. A few of the trees in the garden were planted in honor of deceased loved ones. The result was a place that exuded tranquility, giving center stage to the many works in Hoogendijk's collection.

Even though she loves her current home in the Dutch capital, Hoogendijk fondly thinks back of the place where she started sculpting. It is where it all began.

Cast-concrete floors and white walls and ceilings form a neutral base for Hoogendijk's vintage furniture and minimalist photography. She covered the white grand piano with poems by her friend Maddy Stolk, printed in the Courier font.

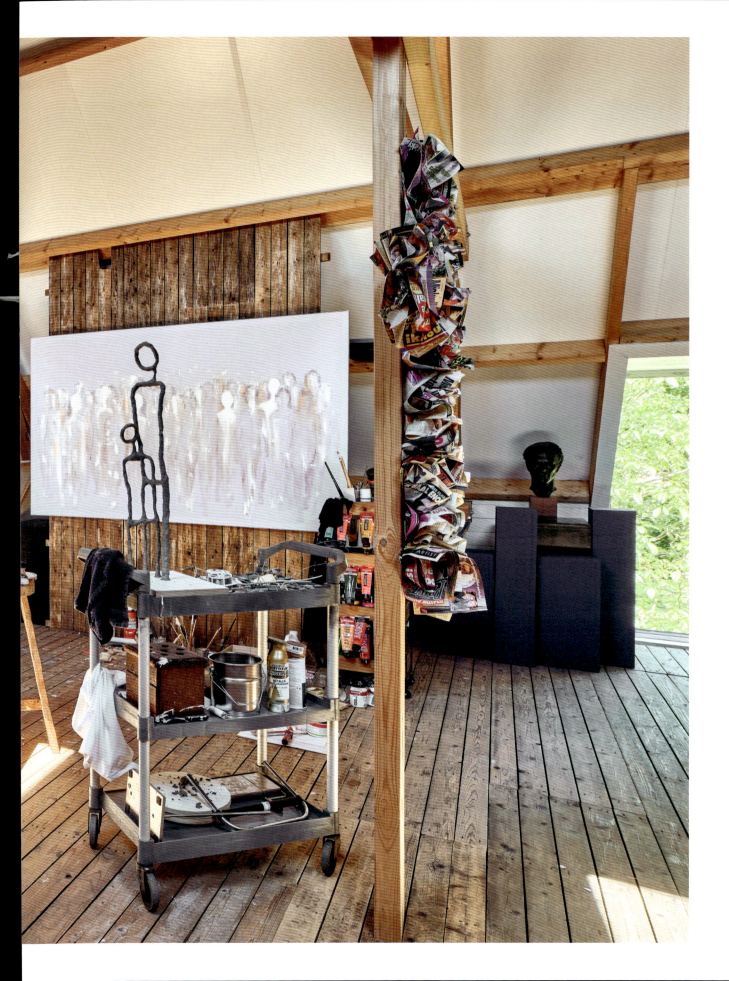

Converted Factory, Tilburg. *Designed by* Henny Guyt & Maicol van den Oetelaar. *Inhabited by* Maicol & Yasmina van den Oetelaar

FANTASY FUN FACTORY

Hidden within a courtyard in Tilburg's historic old town lies a former factory that Maicol and Yasmina van den Oetelaar have transformed into a stunning, loft-style abode. They had been looking for a suitable home for a long time but did not find anything until they stumbled upon a dilapidated workshop in need of complete renovation. Family and friends declared the couple crazy, but they saw potential in the large, bright spaces.

Maicol van den Oetelaar co-owns Vervoort, a furniture company that provides interiors for commercial clients such as restaurants, hotels, vacation parks, and health-care services. Having worked professionally with Henny Guyt of StudiOzo, van den Oetelaar also chose to invite the architect on this private adventure.

Aided by his father and a few friends, van den Oetelaar demolished part of the interior himself. Any building materials released in the process, including wooden beams, were repurposed during the renovation.

A loft now brings light into the heart of the house. Large glass doors give access to a walled courtyard garden that is an oasis of calm at the heart of this lively student city. The residents have even more outdoor space at their disposal, thanks to a large roof terrace above the entrance hall and garage. On the second floor, on either side of the loft, are two bedrooms. Some of the furniture comes from Vervoort, allowing van den Oetelaar to test his company's products in everyday life. After all, the proof is in the pudding.

A void brings daylight deep into the house. The round blue carpet is by Simone Post and the green pouf was designed by Pierre Paulin for Artemide in the 1960s.

Creative Homes
Interiors and Design in the Netherlands

A Book by gestalten & René van der Hulst
Edited by Robert Klanten, René van der Hulst, and François-Luc Giraldeau

Photography by René van der Hulst
Styling by José Martens (pp. 26–35, 72–79, 80–93, 108–127, 152–169, 214–223)
and Marloes Wolfs (pp. 36–45)

Preface, Text, and Captions by David Keuning

Editorial Management by Anna Diekmann

Design, Cover, and Layout by Stefan Morgner

Photo Editor: Madeline Dudley-Yates

Typefaces: GT Alpina by Reto Moser, Sprat by Ethan Nakache

© VG Bild-Kunst, Bonn 2024 for the works of Gerrit Thomas Rietveld (p. 30, 32),
Frans Schrofer (p. 83, 86), Willem Schrofer (p. 89),
Piet Hein Eek (p. 130, 134, 175), and Micky Hoogendijk (p. 202, 203)

Printed by Gutenberg Beuys Feindruckerei, Langenhagen
Made in Germany

Published by gestalten, Berlin 2025
ISBN 978-3-96704-174-3

© Die Gestalten Verlag GmbH & Co. KG, Berlin 2025

All rights reserved. No part of this publication may be reproduced or transmitted in any form or by any means, electronic or mechanical, including photocopy or any storage and retrieval system, without permission in writing from the publisher.

Respect copyrights, encourage creativity!

For more information, and to order books, please visit www.gestalten.com

Die Gestalten Verlag GmbH & Co. KG
Mariannenstrasse 9–10
10999 Berlin, Germany
hello@gestalten.com

Bibliographic information published by the Deutsche Nationalbibliothek.
The Deutsche Nationalbibliothek lists this publication in the Deutsche Nationalbibliografie;
detailed bibliographic data is available online at www.dnb.de

None of the content in this book was published in exchange for payment by commercial parties or designers;
the inclusion of all work is based solely on its artistic merit.

This book was printed on paper certified according to the standards of the FSC®.